Zoom in on WEATHER MAPS

Kathy Furgang

Enslow Publishing
101 W. 23rd Street
Suite 240
New York, NY 10011
USA
enslow.com

WORDS TO KNOW

air pressure The weight of the air.

atmosphere The air around us.

barometer A tool used to measure air pressure.

compass rose A map symbol that shows direction.

forecast A prediction of something that is likely to happen.

humidity The amount of moisture in the air.

isobars Lines on a weather map that show areas of air pressure.

legend A tool on a map that explains what map symbols mean.

meteorologist A person who studies the weather.

precipitation Any moisture, such as rain or snow, that falls from the sky.

satellites Machines in space that circle Earth and are used to track weather.

CONTENTS

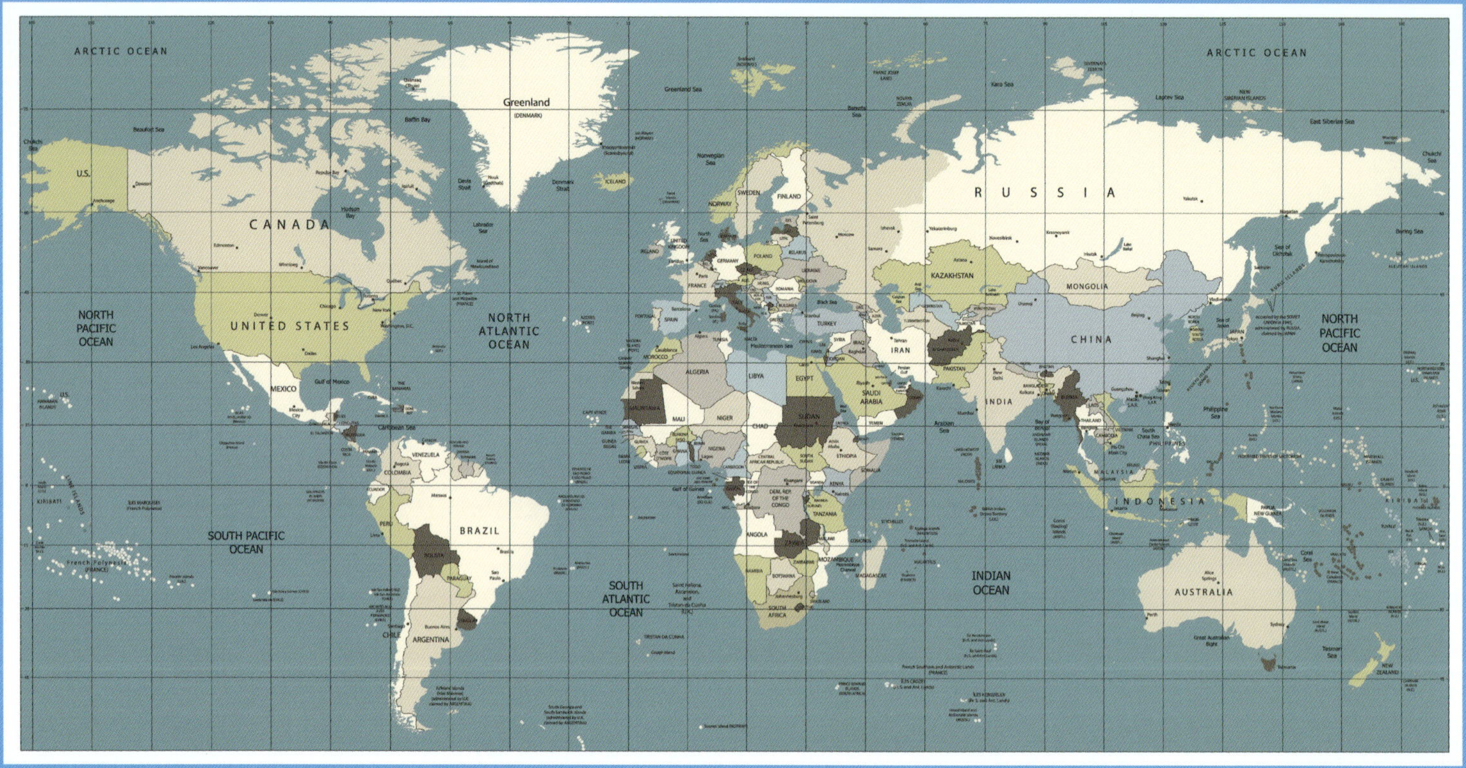

Each map tells us about a certain place, whether it is a small town or the entire world.

A World of Maps

What tool would be most helpful for finding your way when you are lost? A map! Maps help us understand our world. They help us travel through new areas. They label countries, states, roads, oceans, and rivers. Some maps give information about the weather in an area. Some even show what plants grow in a certain area.

Where Are the Roads?

Weather maps do not often show roads. Weather maps may show state boundaries and city names, but the focus is on the weather and conditions of the atmosphere.

A map is a picture of an area on Earth. Maps can even be pictures of the entire world. This book will teach you how to read and understand a weather map.

How Maps Are Alike

Most maps have some features in common. Many maps have a legend. A legend is a box with symbols that shows you how to read the information on the map. A legend may show what

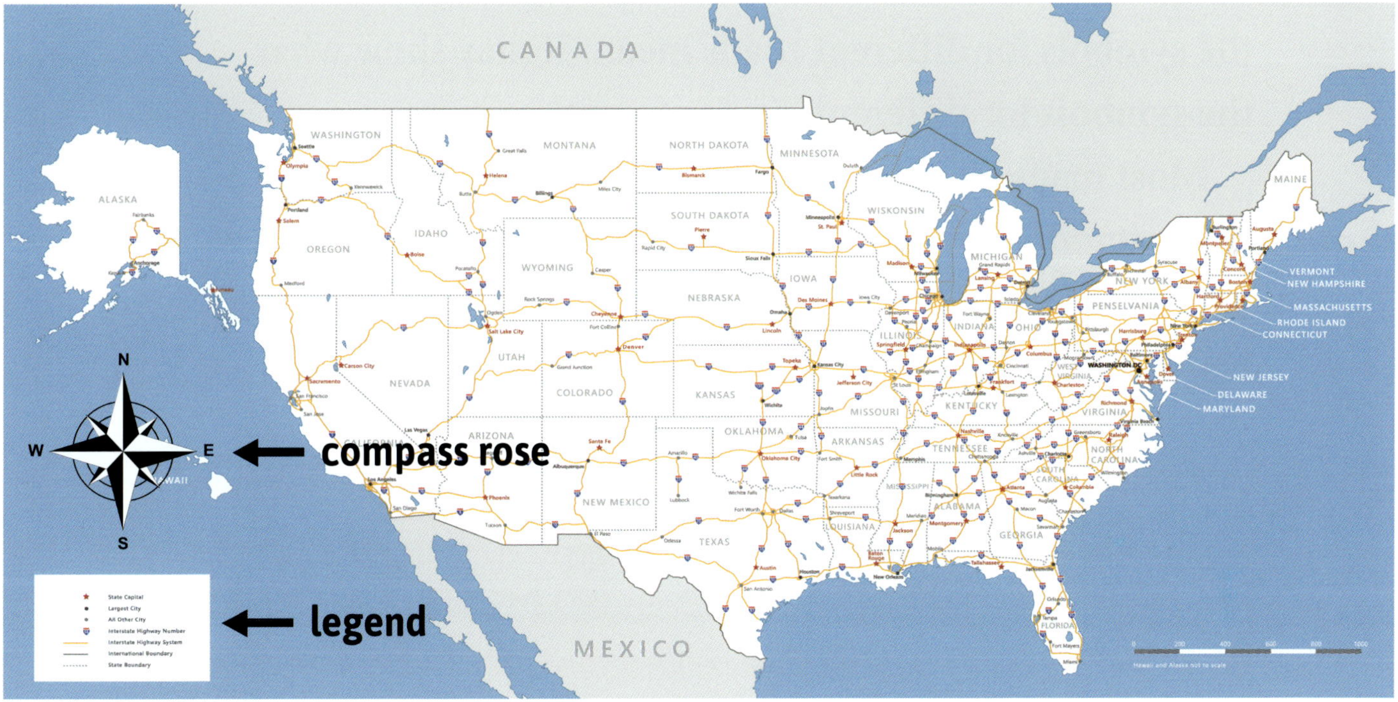

This map of the United States includes a legend that explains map symbols and a compass rose that shows direction.

the symbols for different roads mean. It may show what the symbols for different kinds of weather mean.

Most maps also have a compass rose. That's a tool for understanding the directions on a map. The compass rose has arrows labeled N, S, E, and W. These stand for the four main directions, which are north, south, east, and west.

Understanding Weather Maps

You wake up in the morning and want to know the weather. You might turn on the news to hear the weather report. What's the news reporter pointing to? It's a weather map! Weather is the condition of the air at any time. Weather can be sunny, rainy, cloudy, or windy. The air around us is called the atmosphere. The temperature is how hot or cold the air is.

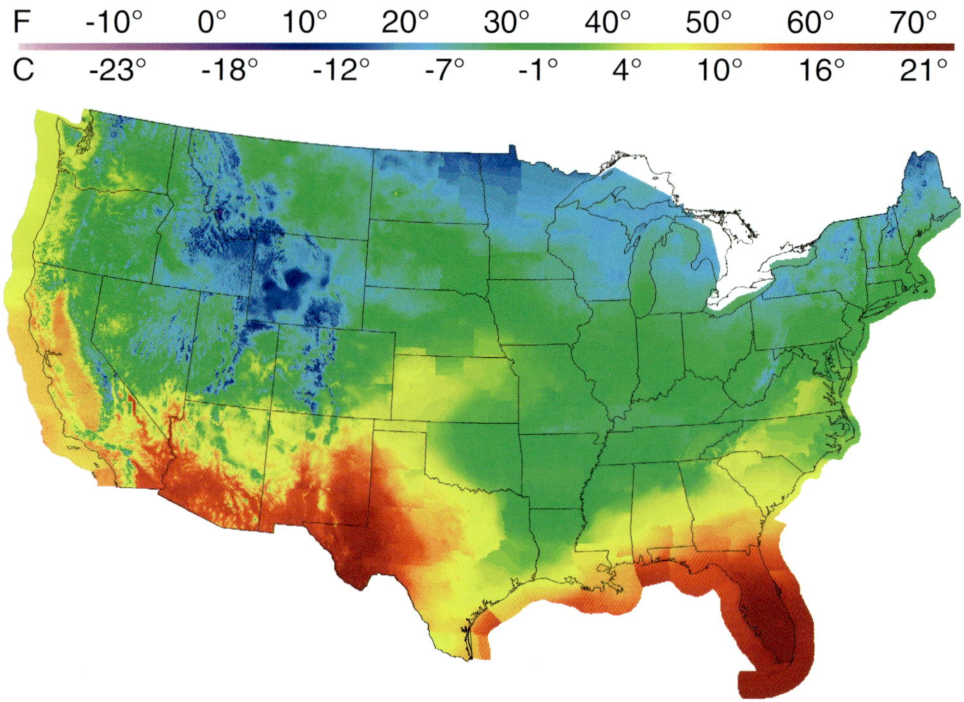

The colors on this map of the United States stand for the temperatures in different areas of the country. The legend on top shows both Fahrenheit and Celsius measurements.

Scientists predict, or make a good guess, about what the weather will be like in the future. This is called a weather forecast. Some weather maps give a forecast. They show what the weather may be like in the next day, days, or week.

Air Pressure

Weather maps use special symbols to show the weather. Air pressure is the force of the weight that air has on us and on Earth. The weather map on page 12 shows air pressure. Areas of high pressure are marked with an H, while areas of low pressure are marked with an L. Changes in air pressure cause the air to move. As the air moves, its temperature changes.

Under Pressure

Air pressure can be high or low. An area of low, or sinking, pressure is likely to form clouds in the sky and cause precipitation. An area of high, or rising, pressure is likely to bring good weather.

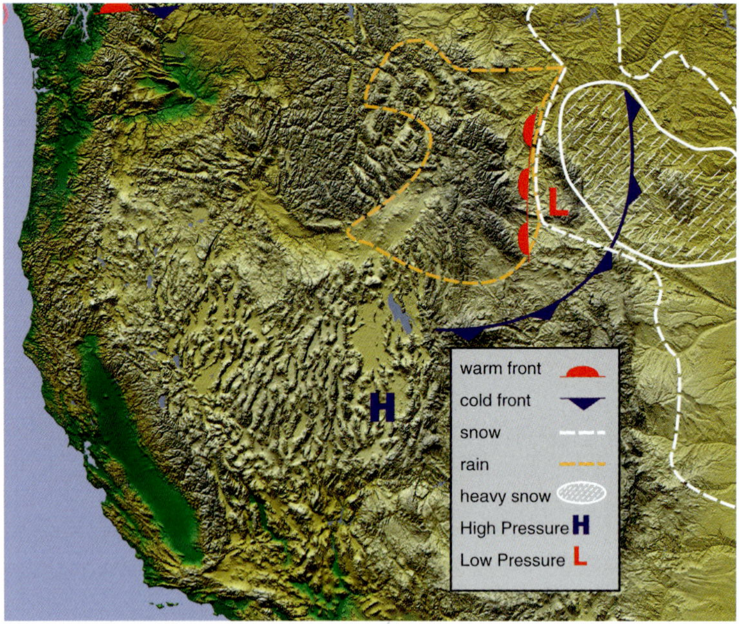

This weather map shows air pressure and precipitation. The legend at the bottom shows what each symbol means and helps us see where it is snowing and where different fronts are moving.

Fronts

A big change in weather is called a front. A large movement of cold air is called a cold front. A large movement of warm air is called a warm front.

Kinds of Weather Maps

One type of weather map shows temperature. In the United States, temperature is measured using the Fahrenheit scale. In other countries, the Celsius scale is used. A temperature map may show the forecast for that day's temperature. This kind of temperature map can help you be ready for that day's weather. Other temperature maps may show the average temperature range for a period of time. This kind of temperature map helps you understand what the weather is usually like in an area. It can also tell you if the forecast for that day is unusual.

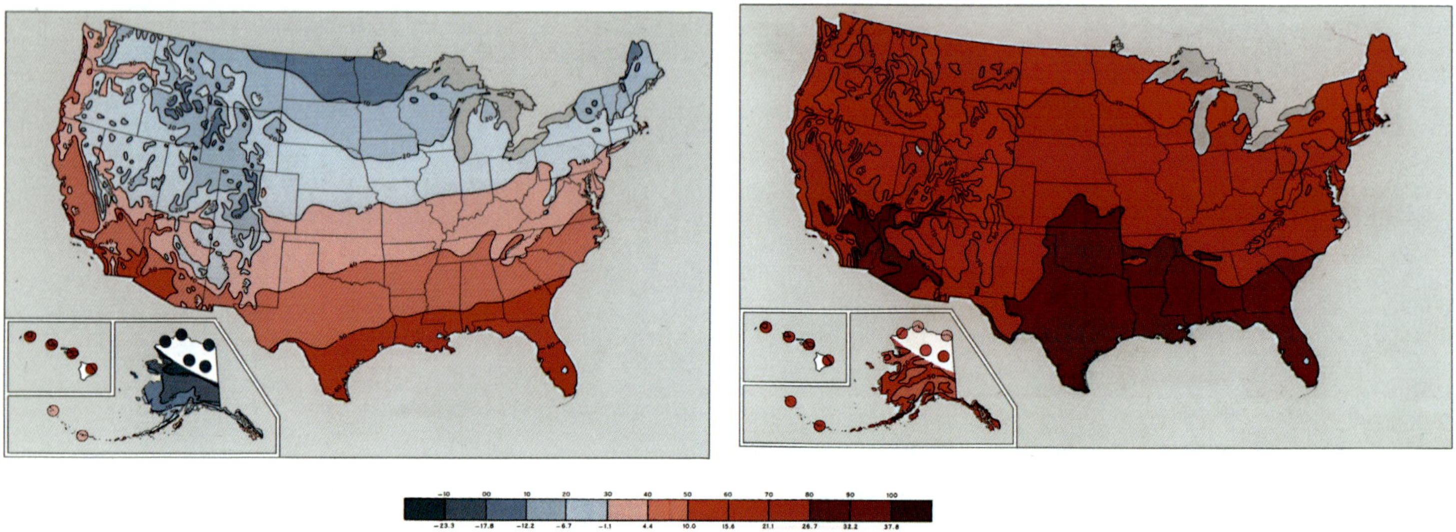

These maps show the difference in temperature from January *(left)* and August *(right)*; areas in blue are the coldest, while red areas are the warmest.

Air Pressure and Precipitation Maps

Some weather maps show precipitation and air pressure. Precipitation maps use symbols to show different kinds of precipitation on the map. For example, snow might be shown by snowflakes, and rain may look like dots. Other precipitation maps use letters to show precipitation. For example, R may stand for rain, and SN may stand for snow.

Some air pressure maps use the letter H for high pressure areas and L for low pressure areas. Other air pressure maps use isobars. An isobar is a line drawn on the weather

This air pressure map shows isobars, which connect areas that have similar pressure.

ZOOM IN ON WEATHER MAPS

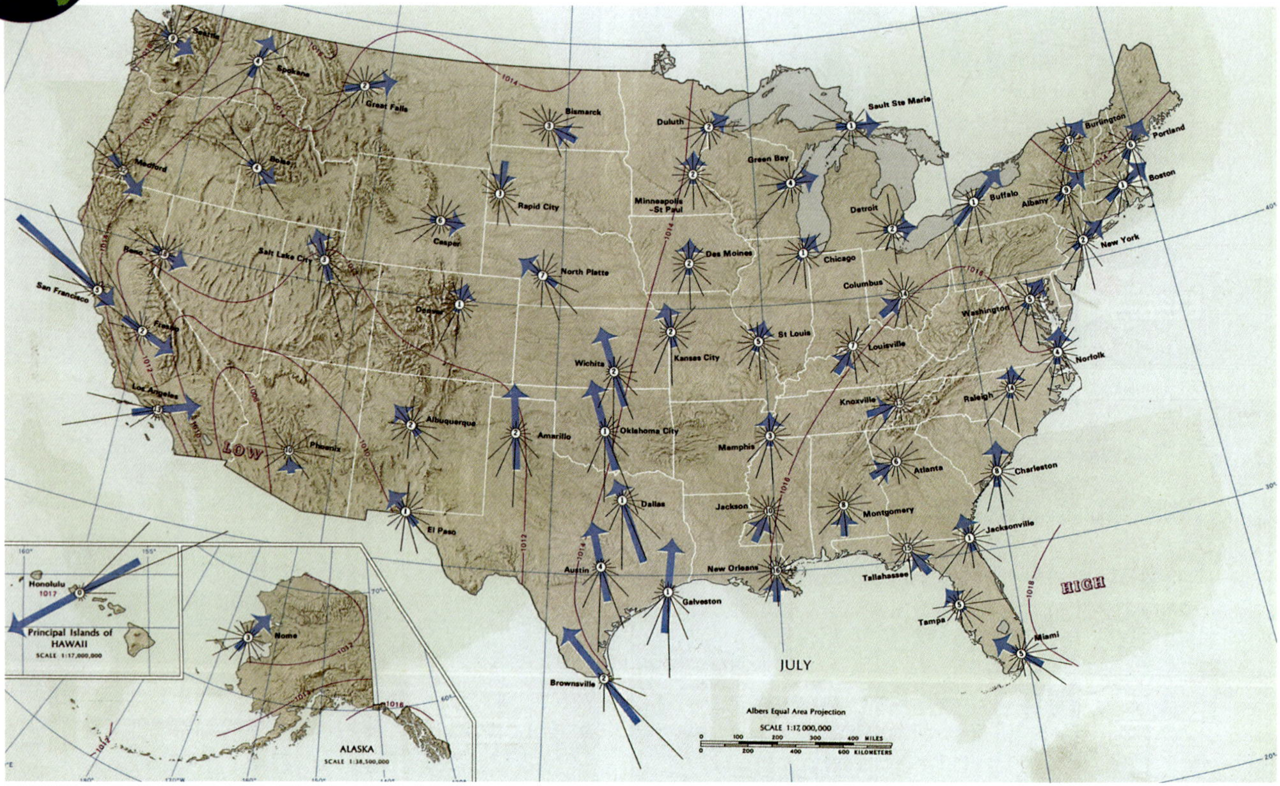

A weather map like this one tells us how fast the wind is blowing and in what direction. The shape at the end of the symbols (called a barb) shows the direction from which the wind is coming.

map that connects areas of similar pressure. The closer an isobar is to the low pressure area, the lower the pressure. The closer an isobar is to the high pressure area, the higher the air pressure.

Direction and Wind

Understanding directions can help you understand wind as a part of weather. For example, a west wind blows from the west toward the east. If you were to trace the direction of a west wind on the map with your finger, it would move from the left to the right.

Windy Weather

Wind plays a big part in severe weather. A hurricane is a storm that has wind speeds more than 75 miles per hour. Most hurricanes start over warm ocean water.

Studying Weather

Meteorologists are scientists who study weather. They use tools to help them make weather forecasts. For example, a **barometer** measures air pressure. Meteorologists try to predict what kind of weather is coming by studying changes in barometric pressure and wind direction.

Meteorologists also make long-term weather forecasts. To do this, they rely on the idea that weather generally travels from west to east in the United States. For example, if it is

Today, meteorologists use computer weather maps that help them make a more accurate forecast.

raining in Ohio, the rain will usually move east toward Pennsylvania.

Making Weather Maps

There are thousands of weather stations around the world. These are places where information about weather is collected. Weather stations can be found on special balloons, ships, airplanes, and buildings.

Meteorologists use the information from weather stations to help forecast the weather. They look at barometer and temperature readings, precipitation, cloud cover, wind direction, and humidity. Humidity is a measure of the amount of water present in the air.

Using Satellites

Satellites are another tool used for collecting weather information. Satellites

Forecast by Satellite

A satellite is a spacecraft that circles Earth. The satellite sends and receives signals about weather, communication, and transportation. There are thousands of satellites in space at any one time.

take pictures of the weather as it appears from space. Satellites help track storms, such as hurricanes. Weather maps are made from the pictures satellites take. The more scientists study the weather, the more we can learn by reading weather maps!

These weather tools are part of a weather station in Iceland. The instruments can measure things like wind speed, temperature, and humidity.

ACTIVITY: WHAT'S THE FORECAST?

Look at the weather map on page 23. Answer each question, using the color legend on the lower left to help you. Remember that high pressure usually means fair weather and light winds, while a low pressure system can mean stormy weather with heavy winds.

1. Is Florida showing high air pressure or low air pressure? What kind of weather would you guess they are having?
2. What kind of weather should people in central Texas prepare for?
3. What is the general weather in the middle of the country? Are they seeing high pressure or low pressure?
4. What kind of weather will the Northwest (Oregon and Washington) be seeing?

Take it a step further! Watch the weather report on the television news. Is your area experiencing a high or low pressure system? What sort of weather will be coming your way in the next few days? See if the meteorologist is correct!

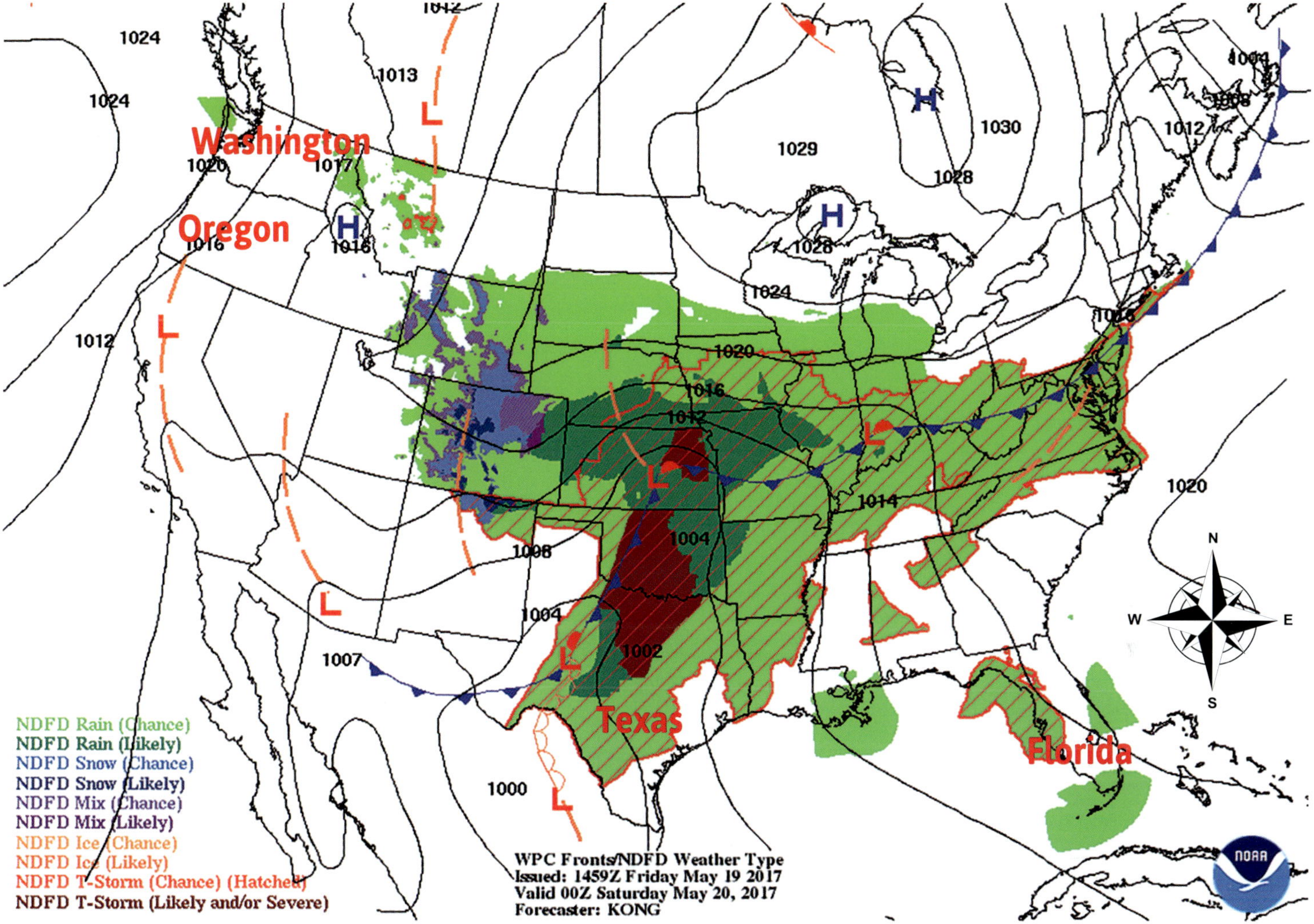
Washington
Oregon
Texas
Florida
NDFD Rain (Chance)
NDFD Rain (Likely)
NDFD Snow (Chance)
NDFD Snow (Likely)
NDFD Mix (Chance)
NDFD Mix (Likely)
NDFD Ice (Chance)
NDFD Ice (Likely)
NDFD T-Storm (Chance) (Hatched)
NDFD T-Storm (Likely and/or Severe)
WPC Fronts/NDFD Weather Type
Issued: 1459Z Friday May 19 2017
Valid 00Z Saturday May 20, 2017
Forecaster: KONG
N
S
E
W
NOAA

LEARN MORE

Books

Balkan, Gabrielle. ***The 50 States: Explore the U.S.A. with 50 Fact-Filled Maps!*** New York, NY: Wide Eyed Editions, 2015.

Mizielinska, Aleksandra, and Daniel Mizielinski. ***Maps***. Somerville, MA: Big Picture Press, 2013.

Smithsonian Children's Illustrated Atlas. London, UK: Dorling Kindersley, 2016.

Websites

BrainPop Jr.

jr.brainpop.com/socialstudies/geography/readingmaps/

Play games and take quizzes as you learn to read maps.

National Geographic Kids Atlases

www.nationalgeographic.com/kids-world-atlas/maps.html

Learn about different types of maps by exploring them interactively.

INDEX

Published in 2018 by Enslow Publishing, LLC.
101 W. 23rd Street, Suite 240, New York, NY 10011

Library of Congress Cataloging-in-Publication Data
Names: Furgang, Kathy, author.
Title: Zoom in on weather maps / Kathy Furgang.
Description: New York, NY : Enslow Publishing, 2018. | Series: Zoom in on maps | Includes bibliographical references and index. | Audience: K-3.
Identifiers: LCCN 2017018938| ISBN 9780766092242 (library bound book) | ISBN 9780766094321 (pbk.) | ISBN 9780766094338 (6 pack)
Subjects: LCSH: Maps—Juvenile literature. | Weather—Maps—Juvenile literature.
Classification: LCC GA105.6 .F87 2018 | DDC 551.5022/3—dc23
LC record available at https://lccn.loc.gov/2017018938

Printed in the United States of America

To Our Readers: We have done our best to make sure all website addresses in this book were active and appropriate when we went to press. However, the author and the publisher have no control over and assume no liability for the material available on those websites or on any websites they may link to. Any comments or suggestions can be sent by email to customerservice@enslow.com.

Portions of this book originally appeared in *Weather Maps* by Ian F. Mahaney.

Photos Credits: Cover, p. 1 Harvepino/Shutterstock.com; cover, p. 1 (background) pop_jop/DigitalVision Vectors/Getty Images; pp. 2, 3, 22, back cover dynamic/Shutterstock.com; p. 4 frees/Shutterstock.com; pp. 5, 9, 13, 18 Suz7/Shutterstock.com; pp. 6, 8, 12, 16, 20 gst/Shutterstock.com; p. 7 © iStockphoto.com/shoo_arts; pp. 10, 23 National Oceanic and Atmospheric Administration/National Weather Service; p. 12 Greg Tucker adapted from NASA/JPL – Caltech; pp. 14, 16 Library of Congress Geography and Map Division; p. 15 Frank Fiedler/Shutterstock.com; p. 19 Boston Globe/Getty Images; p. 21 subtik/E+/Getty Images.